Unicorn Handwriting and Number Tracing Coloring Book for Girls Ages 4-8

Sofia Logan & School Princess Press

ISBN: 9798649758772

Copyright © 2020
All rights reserved. No part of this publication may be reproduced, distributed, or transmitted in any form or by any means, including photocopying, recording, or other electronic or mechanical methods, without the prior written permission of the publisher, except as permitted under Section 107 or 108 of the 1976 United States Copyright without permission request from the author.
E-Mail: Lerner.Book@gmail.com

A

Ava

Brooklyn

D

Delilah

dear

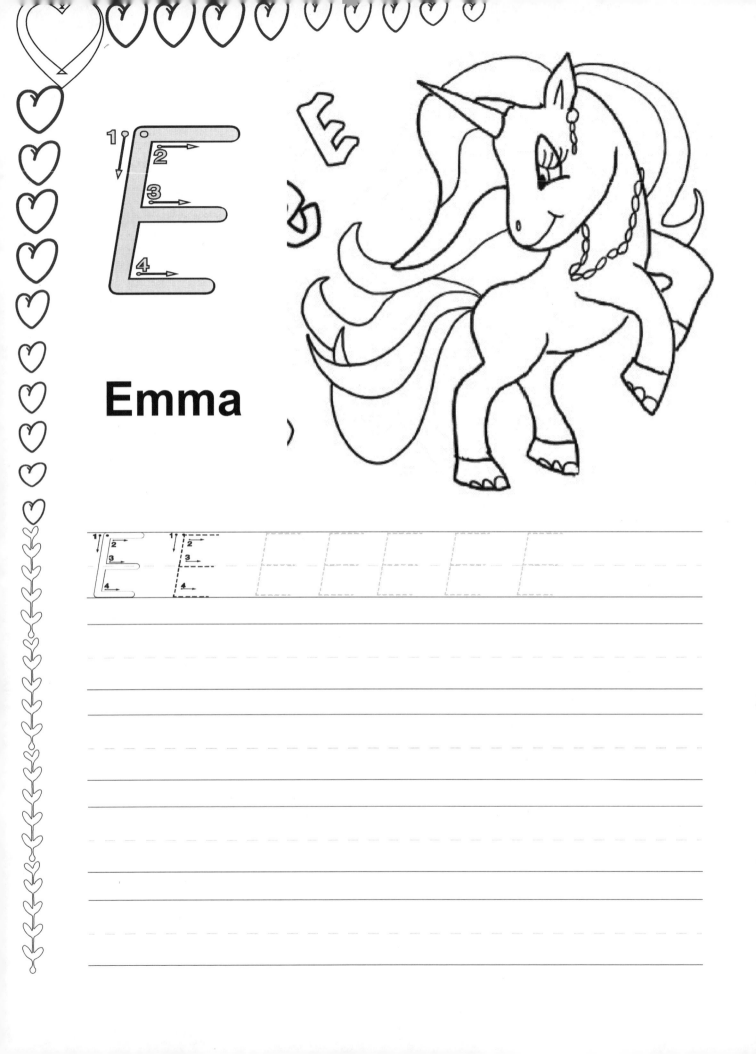

Emma

excellent

Faith

f
faithful

f f f f f f f

gorgeous

Harper

handsome

Isabella

Julia

kind

Layla

lovely

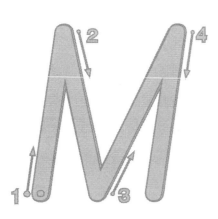

Mia

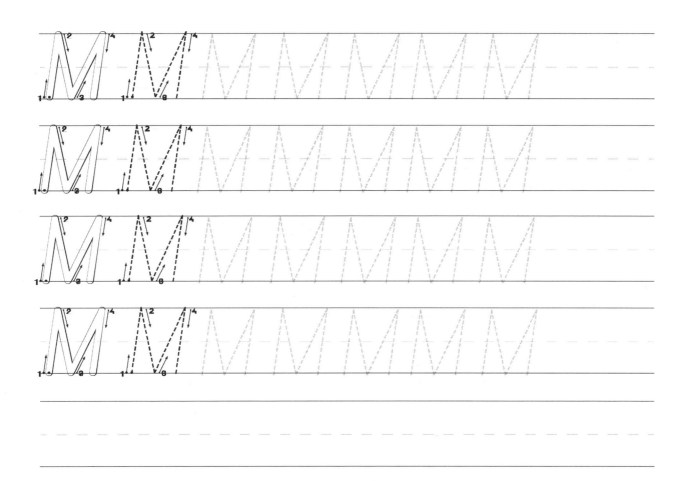

nice

Olivia

O

optimistic

Penelope

perfect

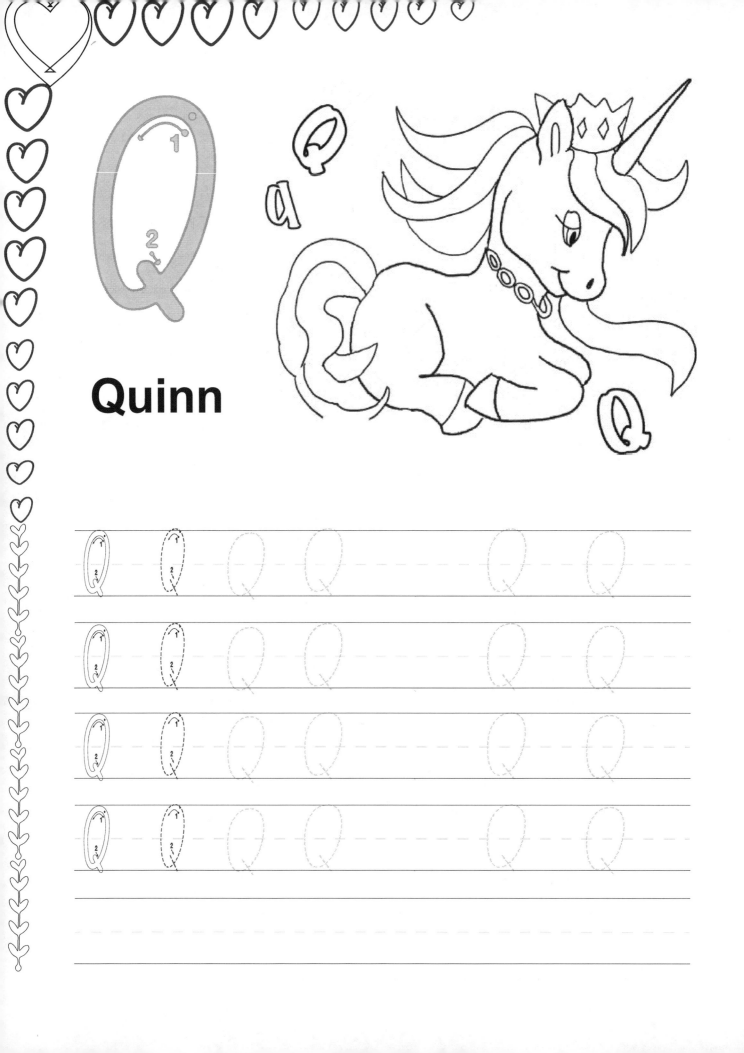

Quinn

queenly

R

Riley

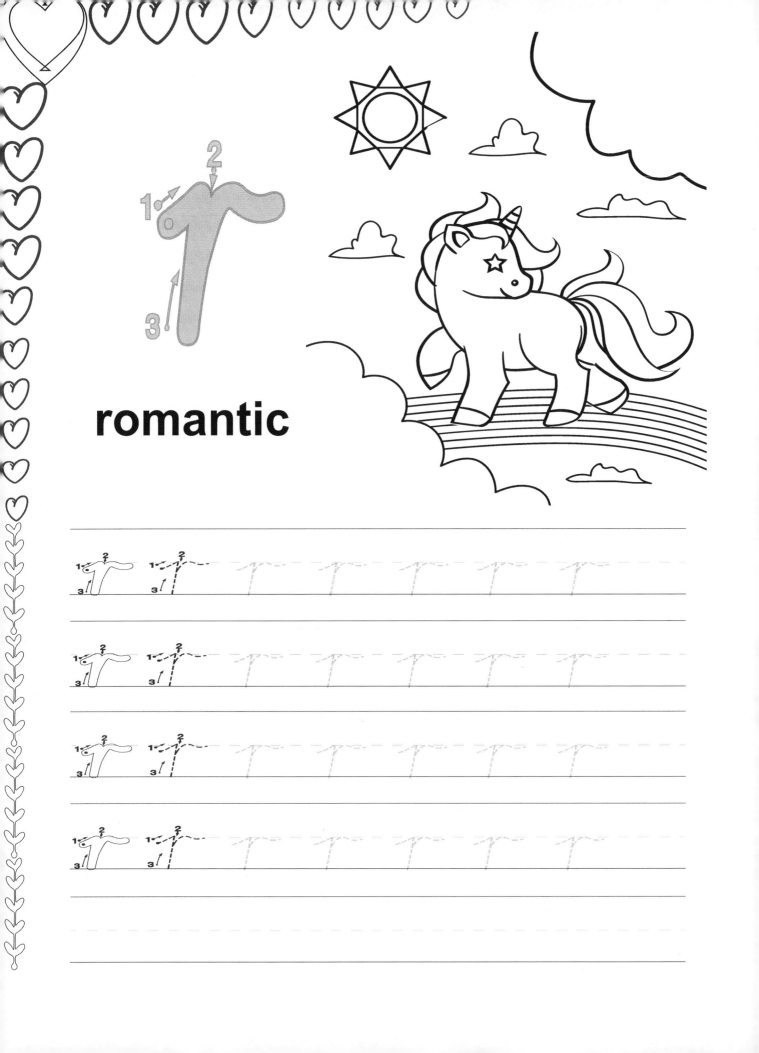

romantic

Sophia

S S S S S S S

superior

Talia

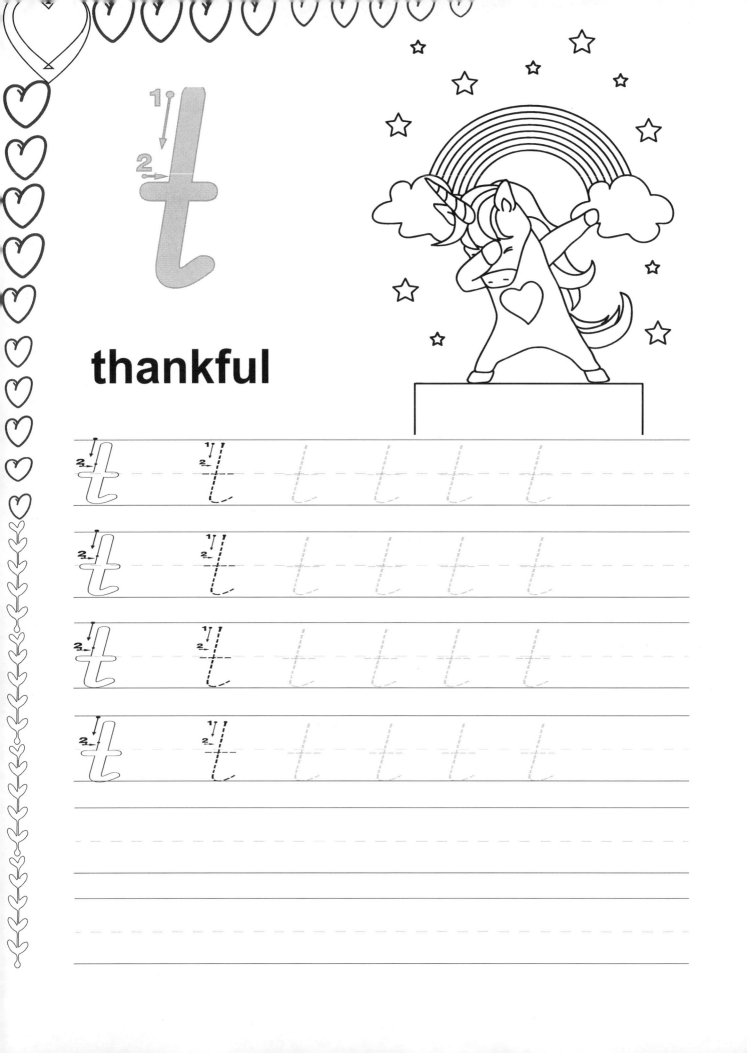

Ursula

unique

valuable

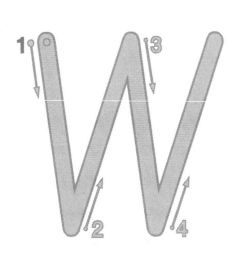

Willow

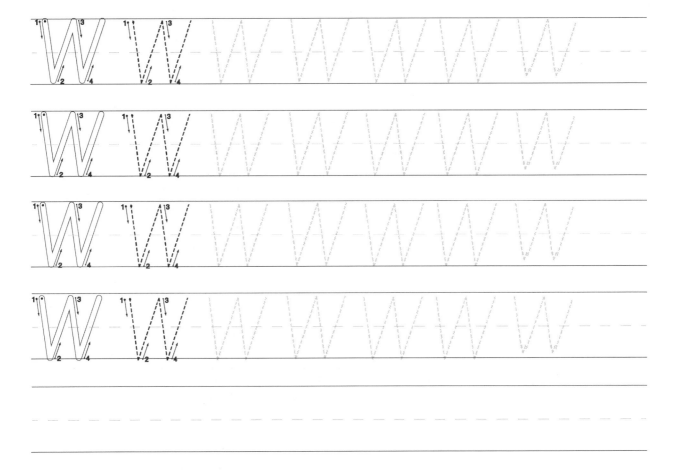

wonderful

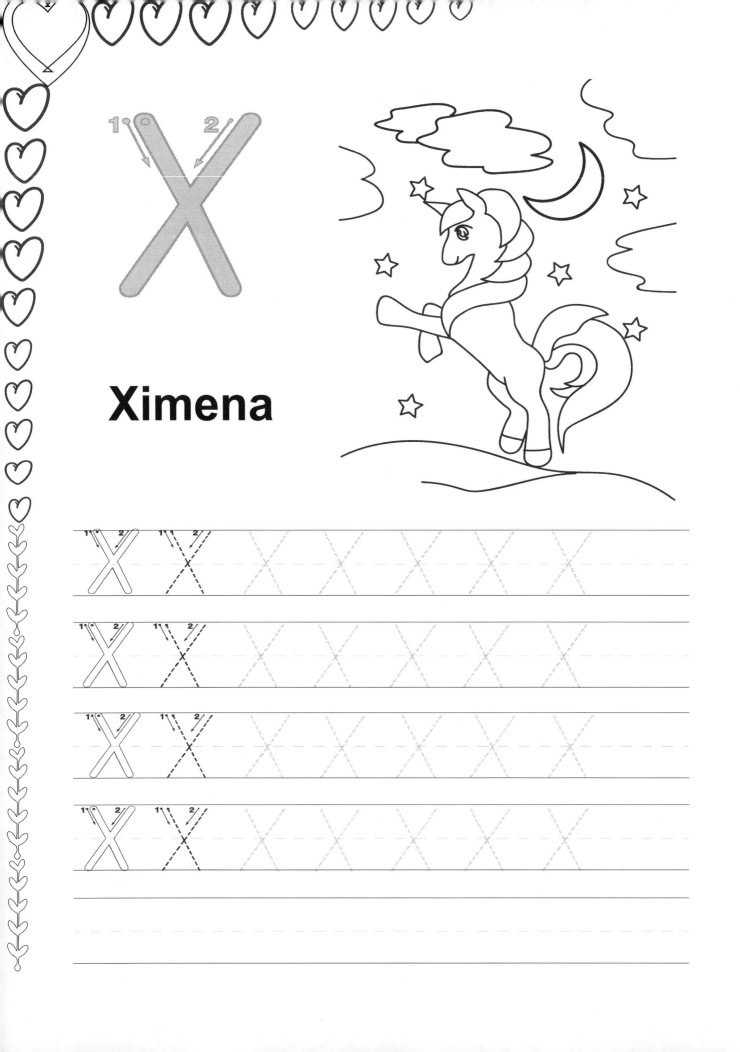

Ximena

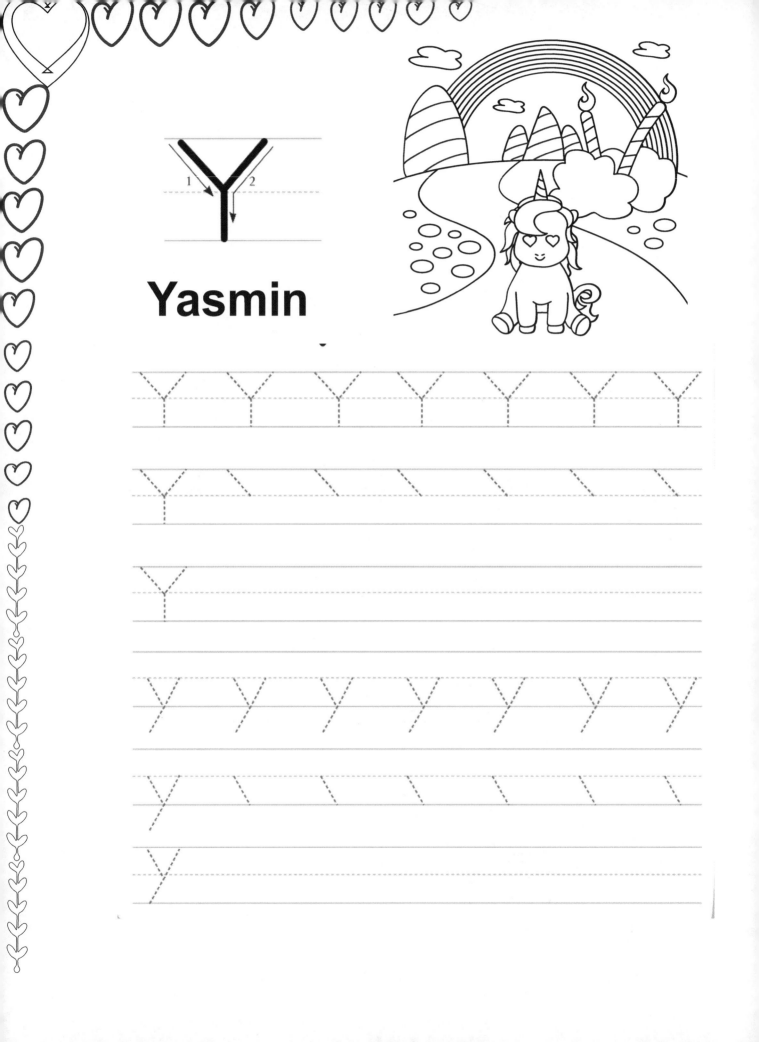

Yasmin

young

Zoe

zaftig

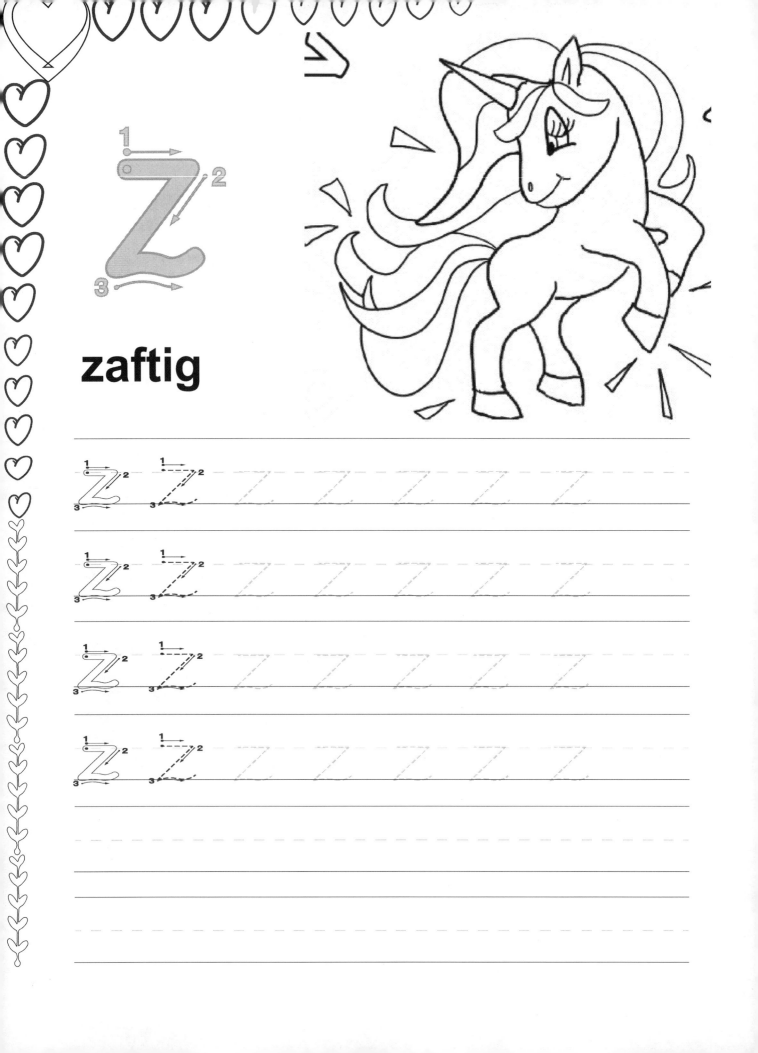

1

One

2

Two

3
Three

4

Four

Five

6

Six

6

7

Seven

9
Nine

Ten

10

10

10

For every review on Amazon we donate **2 USD** for girls & women's rights in Afghanistan. In Afghanistan According to the UN, 87% of all women experience at least one form of violence: physical, sexual, psychological or forced marriage, only 15% of women and girls can read.

Made in the USA
Columbia, SC
26 February 2025

54474999R00070